Girls Gone Grape
Celebrating the Girlfriends
In Your Wine Pack

Robin Salls
-Founder Girls Gone Grape, Inc.

Printed in the United States of America
ISBN – 13: 978-0692937723
ISBN – 10: 0692937722

For David and Elle.
Sipping through life is full of bubbles and adventures,
Because you're in it!

CONTENTS

ACKNOWLEDGEMENTS

Thank you to everyone that has sipped along on this adventure called Girls Gone Grape. I am amazed and thrilled with all the support you've shown on our mission to connect and inspire women over adventures and wine. Thank you Elle, my daughter + friend + drinking pal who inspired me to follow my passion into my next chapter. Thank you David, my husband + best friend + bouncer + Guy Gone Grape for supporting me and putting up with a lot of girls' nights out. To Yvette and Jessica for becoming my first GGG Champagne Members…thank you for believing in my dream from day one. Thank you Kristie for the many nights of being my traveling & sipping pal on many adventures! Thank you Laine for believing eyes and many shared sips along the way.

You're all part of the reason for my Dolce Vita! My Sweet Life!

Forward/Avanti

Salute! You're our kind of gal and I know this because not only did you pick up this book, but you're reading it too! Only a sassy, wine loving adventurous woman would be drawn to a book where describing our girlfriends as wine types/varietals comes as second nature as popping those corks! Then, we throw in a few adventures or challenges for you to share with your friends, along with a few cocktail recipes and presto….We've got a book for the woman who understands the importance of inspiring connection, support, well-being and friendships amongst women. Women inspiring women. The inspiration for this book arose from Girls Gone Grape, a community of sassy women, enjoying sassy adventures over sassy wines! Could I use the word "sassy" anymore?

Maybe you're thinking to yourself "what community?" You picked up this book because of its eye catching title and thought it'd be a fun read. Well, you're right! It will be a fun read, but by the end, you might just find yourself running to the nearest Girls Gone Grape chapter because you want to sip with us too! But before we get started, I need to give you a warning, so here goes…

   WARNING: if you're looking for a book backed by statistics and research….STOP reading this minute. The main research that was conducted for this book, if that's what you want to call it, was in the many sips over monthly events throughout the years that I've hosted as the Founder of Girls Gone Grape, Inc. I am not a Sommelier. By choice. I could take the tests and possibly change that status and maybe someday I will, but for now, I'd rather you know I'm a gal like everyone else who enjoys her wine and has broadened her knowledge of it over many sips with family and friends. Practice makes perfect, right? And boy, do I practice.

A little about me and why you should continue reading... I'm a woman who is passionate for wine, food, my family and trying out new adventures, while always finding ways to see things differently. When I designed handbags (one of the ways I tried to define myself over the years) they were named after my girlfriends, so, it was only second nature to start seeing my girlfriends as wine varietals. Yes, sometimes that was easier after a few sips! The closer I looked at characteristics of the wines I love and my friend's personalities, the more I started jokingly referring to them as my wine pack. Why pack? Because I'm also the mom of 4 fur babies all over 50lbs, so I travel in packs! And, in the liquor store I rarely leave with one bottle. My wine shopping is in packs of 3, 6 or 12. Just as I mix up the varietals in my fur pack (Golden Retriever, Black Labrador, Boxer, and Boxer/American Bulldog), I mix up my wine packs. I'll throw in Sauvignon Blanc with a Pinot Grigio along with a Shiraz and a bold Cabernet Sauvignon, and of course, there are always bubbles included because bubbles start everything off right. That's my idea of a wine pack! Bubbles really should be a daily requirement. After all, there are studies out there pointing to wine and champagne being beneficial in many ways. I can attest to their mood enhancing effects, as I feel happier when I'm sharing sips with my loved ones. I can also share that my loved ones appear to be quite happy as well when we're sharing sips. In fact, if you're not sharing sips at my place, then please report me as missing because missing is the only way I won't be pouring sips for you. Plus, we have a gorgeous spare bedroom or two, so safety is always on our minds. We actually have a few friends that keep a spare change of clothes in the closet. You might call your friends your wine club or sisterhood, but you get the idea. Wine and women just naturally pair well together.

> "AND I GET REFILL NUMBER THREE OR FOUR AND THE WINE IS MAKING MY BONES LOOSE AND IT'S GIVING MY HAIR A RED SHEEN AND MY BREASTS ARE BLOOMING AND MY EYES FEEL SULTRY AND WISE AND THE DRESS IS WATER."
> AIMEE BENDER

I've taken my favorite wines, well the top 5 varietals, matched them to personality traits of my friends and realized how important each of these relationships are to me as a woman. Each is valuable in its own way. A nugget of gold, so to speak or as diamonds are said to be a girl's best friend, a shiny, brilliant diamond to be treasured. Then I got to wondering if others looked at their girlfriends this way. You know, through wine glasses?

I had to share my thoughts as they were like the bubbles in a champagne bottle pressuring up against the cork waiting to pop. My hope is you'll smile to yourself as you read this book and discover you have friends that make up your wine pack. You'll laugh as memories pop into your mind of the adventures you've had up till now and hopefully get jazzed up at the thought of the adventures that lay ahead.

Perhaps one or two of our challenges get you pumped up to see what you and your gal pals can come up with. Or, maybe these challenges will help you stretch your comfort zone to get out and meet some new gals. Because if you're not planning more adventures over wine with your gals by the end of this book, then I have definitely not accomplished my desire for this book and why I had to put pen to paper and bring it out of the lock box in my mind. Wine. Women. Friendships. The value of these things cannot be expressed enough.

> **D IS FOR DEMI-SEC**
> **FRENCH TERM MEANING HALF- DRY**
> **TO DESCRIBE A SPARKLING WINE.**

We need our girlfriends in our lives. Which is why this book is interactive giving you a chance through challenges to bring your gals together more often. That said, as we continue, let me give you a quick peek as to how this crazy adventure known as Girls Gone Grape began.

I was a woman who'd stuffed the importance of girlfriend time back into my bra drawer. You know the drawer I'm talking about. The one with your current bras in the front and the forgotten ones in the back, but you really liked them at one point, so you don't want to let them go. That's sort of what had happened to my girlfriend time over the years. At first, it was a priority to spend time with my girlfriends. They were my lifeline, but as life changed and we moved around, had kids and a husband, the girlfriend time got pushed to the back of the list more and more. I wasn't even fully conscious of it until the fall of 2011.

I woke up on my daughter's first day of her senior year of high school realizing that as she was about to embark on a new chapter in her life, so was I. I was going to be Robin again and not just Elle's mom. I had a little bit of an anxiety attack. Okay, I had a pretty big anxiety attack. What did that look like anymore to be Robin? I looked around and realized that my "girlfriends" we're actually moms of her friends and other than our daughter's, we didn't have much, in some cases, anything in common. I can remember thinking, holy crap, I have no girlfriends other than a few and they were out of state. I needed to find some friends that I could share things with and well, I love wine. It seemed logical to join a wine meet up group to meet other women who shared this passion. Right? Little did I know this was about to take me on the adventure of a lifetime, throwing my roadmap out the window…..I couldn't find a group I felt part of after several visits because I grew up with wine being fun and celebratory, not stuffy and rigid, which is what I was finding in the groups I visited. They felt like they were putting rules on wine. Rather or not they actually were, that's how they felt to me. Perception means everything, right?

Feeling disappointed, my husband asked why I didn't just start my own group? What a concept? Silly, faithful and supportive man that he is, here we are years later with Girls Gone Grape, Inc. being a core part of our lives. I'd forgotten how important those outside female relationships can be for the benefit of myself and my relationship with my husband. I'd forgotten that women could inspire one another, rather than compete with one another in a society where too many are breaking each other down, rather than lifting each other up. Girls Gone Grape was born out of a need for friendship with other women, but Girls Gone Grape has become so much more for myself and others as we've been blessed with friendships that have opened our eyes and inspired us.

I hope you'll feel inspired to celebrate your friendships or make new ones at the end of this short read. Maybe you needed a reminder of the importance of girlfriends, as I did. Or, maybe you already knew that and this just makes you smile as you're reminded of your girlfriends. Whatever your reason for reading, thank you for taking the time to share a part of this journey with me. One last note…you'll find my favorite quotes and wine terms splashed throughout these pages. Know there is no rhyme or reason to their placement. Much like my adventures in life, they just popped in place where it felt right. Enjoy.

Salute,

Robin Salls

Robin Salls
Founder + President

What Defines A Girl Gone Grape?

She's Confident, Intelligent & Independant

She Knows Her Glass Is Always Half Full & Ready For More

She's Spunky & Full of Sass

She Lives By The Motto "Sip On Life & Enjoy Every Moment"

She Rocks Her Own Signature Style

She Surrounds Herself With Positive People

She Celebrates Life & Dances In The Rain

She Honors & Takes care Of Herself

She Indulges In Wine, Cocktails & Beer Because She Can

Girls Gone Grape

What Defines A Girl Gone Grape?

- **She's Confident, Intelligent & Independent –** She knows what she wants and isn't afraid to speak her mind or go after it. Is there anything more beautiful than a woman who is confident and not afraid to show it? I don't think so.

- **She Knows Her Glass is Always Half Full and Ready for More –** She's optimistic. Even during bumps in the road she always believes there is room for more out of life! Especially more wine! She always looks forward and doesn't dwell on the past.

- **She's Spunky & Full of Sass –** She's adventurous, classy and yes, sometimes gives you a bit of sass. Again, she speaks her mind while striving to live the fullest life possible.

- **She Lives by the Motto "Sip on Life and Enjoy Every Moment" –** She knows life goes by too fast, so she takes note of the moment and enjoys it fully. She embraces every moment as if it were her last, so no regrets…She sees, she hears, she listens, she tastes, she speaks.

- **She Rocks Her Own Signature Style –** She's true to herself and her style; whatever that may be at the moment. Maybe it's formal, maybe it's super girly, but it's hers. No cookie cutter looks for this gal. It's her style and she wears it like none other.

- **She Celebrates Life and Dances in the Rain –** She knows that you can't stop the difficult moments, but you can choose to dance in them. You can choose to celebrate them as a part of life's lessons to better things. You can choose to Tango during a storm rather than run for cover.

- **She Surrounds Herself with Positive People** – Positive energy, positive vibe, positive you. Simply put, but it works. She gives herself permission to keep negative energy at a distance, regardless of where it's coming from.

- **She Honors and Takes Care of Herself** – She knows taking care of herself allows her to be her best for those in her life. Selfish isn't in her vocabulary, but recognizing that she needs "self-time" is mandatory for health. Those bubble baths aren't just for getting clean!

- **She Indulges in Wine, Cocktails and Beer because she can** – She understands you should enjoy the things you love because you decide that you can. No one else should get to decide for you. And, "just because"… is sometimes a good enough reason.

> **"DRINK FREELY THE WINE LIFE OFFERS YOU AND DON'T WORRY HOW MUCH YOU SPILL.**
> **MARTY RUBIN**

When I met with the Graphic Designer to create the logo for Girls Gone Grape I had a specific thought in my mind of what she should represent. I wasn't sure what she should look like though. Enter Wayne, a graphic designer in a leads groups I was in who listened intently to my vision, even if he didn't quite grasp the concept of GGG. A week later he came back with a gal in a red dress holding a white wine glass with long, straight blond hair, blue eyes and a big smile. She was cute, in a college style kind of way but she didn't have enough sass. She needed something more, so off to the drawing board he went. I suggested he have a glass or two of wine to inspire him. It always helps me… A week later we got what is now our signature gal who exemplifies the sassy spirit of Girls Gone Grape. I believe we all have that little black dress that makes us feel like a sassy rock star when we wear it. Yes, you are expecting the

V IS FOR VARIETAL
TERM USED FOR SPECIFIC GRAPE NAMES, EX. SYRAH, CHARDONNAY, MERLOT, ETC. IN MOST REGIONS FOR A WINE TO QUAIFY AS A VARIETAL, IT MUST BE PRODUCED FROM 85% OFTHEGRAPE LISTED ON THE LABEL; THE U.S. IS A BIT LOOSER AT 75% MINIMUM

paparazzi to be jumping out of the bushes because you look that hot! Let's raise a toast to feeling like rock stars even when we're not in those little black dresses! We should feel that way daily about ourselves!

GGG Signature Cocktail & Recipe

Do you have a signature style? I mean one that you truly own? Every woman should channel her own Coco Chanel, Audrey Hepburn, Madonna or Miranda Lambert style. Those are women who owned or own their styles, no excuses! One of my signature looks are the champagne necklaces you'll catch me wearing that make it clear how passionate I am about wine. Just ask anyone who knows me and they'll tell you that you can spot me in the room by the cork necklace around my neck! I've got a cork necklace to color coordinate with any outfit! Heck yes, it's an awesome reason to keep champagne in the house. Bring home a new outfit, pop open a bottle of champagne and create another necklace! Wine is my lifestyle and I make no apologies for my signature style.

You know where I'm going with this, right? Girls Gone Grape needed a signature cocktail, especially if I'm going to be talking about signature styles. Plus, years of gals asking if Girls Gone Grape actually had our own signature cocktail were getting tiresome, so I decided to kick off 2016 with a fabulous event. One that brought the gals of our founding chapter together in Northern Colorado to create a unique wine based cocktail.

I could have simply created a drink myself, but what fun would be in that….Plus, I didn't really know where to begin other than with wine. I wasn't a bartender after all. Luckily, in my business I'm fortunate to know lots of Bar and Restaurant owners to turn to in my times of need. And yes, those times of need happen quite regularly when you host events based on women and wine! I need an excuse not to drink with the girls these days! Please don't hate me because I love what I do.

That said, over 30 gals joined us at Generations Wine & Martini Bar in Loveland, Colorado to create our signature cocktail. Erin B., the owner welcomed us for dinner and a bartending 101 course followed by playing around the bar and creating our custom cocktail. As the pro, Erin had some basic starting points for us. She'd created three base cocktails that were wine infused for us to get started with; a sangria, a champagne cocktail and a mint julep. Let me tell you how helpful that was! She let us play to our hearts desire which isn't easy for a room full of women. Shout Outs To Generations Wine and Martini Bar! They will forever be a favorite spot for Girls Gone Grape to sip with the gals!

> ## "EVERYTHING'S BETTER WITH SOME WINE IN THE BELLY."
> ## TYRION LANNISTER

Let me paint a picture for you; 30 plus women huddled around the bar, sampling drinks, adding and removing ingredients, voting as a group on favorites…yes, women actually working together and coming up with what is now known at the Girls Gone Grape Mint Julep, our signature cocktail. A refreshing twist on a favorite Southern style whiskey cocktail. I thought it might be fun for you to sip on this cocktail as you sit back, kick your heels off and start your adventure with us!

The oaked chardonnay is the secret to this cocktail, so be sure you choose an "oaked" chardonnay. That might sound funny as you expect Chardonnay to be oaked, but more and more wineries are creating "unoaked" versions as well, so make sure your bottle doesn't say "unoaked." The oaked Chardonnay acts as the hearty part of our drink that in a typical mint julep is the whiskey. It's light, refreshing and I love that we've created our own wine cocktail! Enjoy!

GGG Mint Julep
A Signature Cocktail Created By Girls Gone Grape

Muddled Mint
3 oz. Oaked Chardonnay
1 oz. Simple Syrup
2 oz. Soda or Seltzer Water

Muddle mint in shaker, add Chardonnay & Simple Syrup and shake. Add Soda or Seltzer water and pour into sugar rimmed martini or wine glass. Use lemon around the rim and dip glass in fine sugar. For extra fun add green food coloring to sugar! Garnish with mint leaf. Enjoy!

www.girlsgonegrape.com

YOU'RE CHALLENGE - Create your own girlfriends signature cocktail that represents your pack. For example, if you all enjoy champagne, why not make a signature champagne cocktail? You provide the champagne while inviting everyone to bring their favorite embellishment. Perhaps that's a flavored schnapps, vodka or other alcohol, fresh berries, etc. Then set up an area to display all the options to play around with and start pouring the champagne. Have some fun! Try things you might not expect to go with champagne and you might just be surprised. Then share your cocktail recipe with us over at info@girlsgonegrape.com and we'll send you some fun GGG swag for you and your gal pals. We'll also share your recipe (giving your pack the credit on our member's site).

T IS FOR TERROIR
FRENCH FOR GEOGRAPHICAL CHARACTERISTICS UNIQUE TO A GIVEN VINEYARD

The Champagne Girlfriend

Bubbles are some of my favorite sips! They're effervescent, lively, celebratory and always worth the sipping pleasure.   That describes my Champagne girlfriends! They're lively, celebratory and always worth the friendships! Life wouldn't be a party without these gals. Celebrities that come to mind that I believe to be Champagne gals…Cameron Diaz, Michelle Pfeiffer, Rachel McAdams or how about a few classics like Sophia Loren, Marilyn Monroe or Audrey Hepburn! I'm a huge movie buff, so be prepared for me to throw some names out as you read along. Champagne girlfriends just really know how to pop! They just have a synergy to them that is hard to describe.

3 Key Inspirations from These Girlfriends:

- You Challenge yourself to be your best! People say to hang with those you admire or have strengths you desire to build within yourself; to surround yourself with those that feed your soul and bring more of what you want into your life. Who doesn't want more bubbles? These relationships energize us.
- You're reminded of the impact living positively can have! It's hard to be negative around these friends. They help you find your happy space, sometimes by just reminding you to stay focused on the positive as they do.
- You appreciate and live in the moment! If you take just one trait from them, let it be living in the moment fully. Make eye contact. Really listen when being spoken too. Love fully.

You can spot a Champagne girlfriend the minute she walks into a room. She's bubbly, friendly and energetic. People are drawn to her smile because she's got a smile for everyone. Her glass is always overflowing. Not because it's never empty, but because she chooses to celebrate life day to day. She appreciates every moment and lives in every moment. She's funny, she's lovable and she's ready to step up to the plate at any moment. You know who I'm talking about. She's the friend that knows the right words and when to be silent. The friend who will jump off the zip line platform with you. She has that fun spark that keeps you on your toes when she's around. She's bursting with ideas and is your chatty Cathy friend. She's like the sun, always burning bright and while sometimes you might need a break in the shade to cool down, you're always drawn back to the warmth of her heart.

There I was listening to our zip line instructor telling us the way to get the fastest run on the zip line is to let go of the handle and basically pull your legs up and wrap them with your arms as if you were doing a cannonball jump into a pool. That's the fastest way to get across the tree lines at some of the highest zip lines in Colorado and my nerves were tingling as I prepared to step to the platform for my very first zip line run in my life. Elle was going to video tape this adventure for me before her turn. She said to me as I hooked into my equipment that there was no way I would cannonball across the entire line....I didn't have the guts. She even had the nerve to bet me tequila shots that I wouldn't do it. Now, if you know me, you know if I'm not sipping wine, you'll probably find me doing tequila shots! Bets laid and off I went. During the recording, you can hear her saying "Oh my god, she's actually doing it. Look at her go. She did it! Way to go mama!." Yes, one of my closest champagne girlfriends is my daughter, Elle.

Friends take on many forms and I'm fortunate to have a champagne girlfriend in my daughter. I had to wait till she was 21 to share the wine and tequila, but she was worth the wait! She inspires me with her love of life attitude and is always up for trying something new with her "all in" spirit towards life. They say having a daughter means you always have a best friend. While that may be hard to believe during those teen years, I can tell you from personal experience how fabulous it is to share sips with my girl now!

Angie is another friend whose energy I can't seem to get enough of. We met on a random night when my husband and I were wandering around a market of various vendors. He'd wandered off as I was checking out some wine gadgets for sale, when he suddenly came up and grabbed me saying I had to meet this woman who makes alcoholic cupcakes. Cupcakes with alcohol? Yes, I'm in! Please, may I have another? Needless to say, we've had numerous events pairing her treats with wine! And every time she delights with her energy and enthusiasm. She's passionate, fun and stays positive always...even when she's hosting our group and the air conditioning decides to go out and the garage door to her commercial kitchen is not opening! She's a single mother who's following her passion and created a business out of it. What a message she sends to her kids. She inspires me too. All I can say is that everything is better with cupcakes and Angie!

There are too many friends to mention that fall under the champagne category who inspire me daily and I am thankful for each and every one of them. I bet you're thinking about a few of your Champagne girlfriends' right about now.

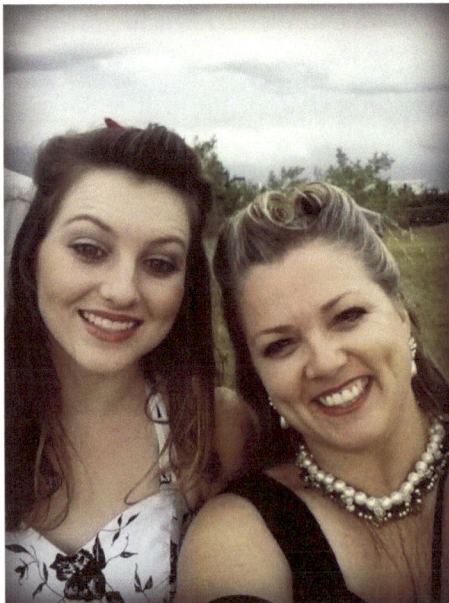

YOU'RE CHALLENGE: Name 3 of your Champagne Girlfriends right off the top of your head. Email us their names at info@girlsgonegrape.com and give us one word that describes them and we'll enter you into our monthly drawing to win a GGG Girlfriends Night In basket! Be sure to tell us they're your Champagne GF's!

List them here and what they've brought into your life:

_____

_____

_____

_____

_____

_____

_____

_____

_____

_____

_____

A IS FOR ACIDITY
THE LIVELINESS AND CRISPNESS IN WINE THAT ACTIVATES OUR SALIVARY GLANDS.

Girls Night Out – 5 Reasons You Can't Live Without Them

Yes! You can't live without regular girl's nights out regardless of your age! From personal experience I can say that many of us will try to live without them for a while....You can spot those gals. They're the ones staring blankly into their drinks with a pasted smile when they happen to glance up. Don't be THAT girl. She's not the sassy woman you know yourself to be. Girls Night Out should be mandatorily scheduled in your calendar. Start today!

Here's why:

1. **To Blow off Steam and Let Your Hair Down -** Remember the days when you just let loose and didn't give a damn? When you didn't work 40 hours a week under artificial lights and then countless hours feeding and taking care of the family? When your biggest concern was what you were going to wear to go dancing and how your hair looked when you smiled at the hottie across the bar? Sometimes, you just need to channel your 22 year old self and live it up with your gals! Your soul needs to be refreshed regularly.

2. **To Unplug Socially and Reconnect Face to Face –** Yes, social media has made it easier to stay in touch via Facebook, Instagram, twitter, etc... but there's nothing like a good gossip session with the girls. No one can chat like your girls and let's face it, most men out there would rather tango with a python than listen to you go on and on and on...Plus, a hug on snapchat just doesn't have the same effect as the hug in person. Sometimes, you just need to experience the moments together and not be worried about who's "liked" your recent post.

3. **To Remind You to Be True to Yourself –** Your closest girlfriends know the real you. Not the one you play at work or put out there for public consumption. They hold you accountable and call you out on your crap.

They've seen the good, the bad, the ugly, the pretty and they're still here. They are the friends that want nothing from you other than your friendship. They help keep you true to yourself.

4. **To Teach You The Importance Of Balancing Your Time** – Whether you're married, single, mother, no kids... you're getting pulled in all sorts of directions. You start feeling like you're a clown in a circus juggling all those balls and freaking out if you start dropping them. Time with your girlfriends helps to balance you. If you're married, it's a nice reminder that you don't lose yourself completely because you've become part of two. If you're single, it's nice to know that until you find your soulmate or if you don't, that your girlfriends will always be your first soulmates. If you're a mom, it's nice to remember what it feels like to take some time for yourself and still use your first name, at least once a month! No children? It's nice to know life is full of sisters to share moments with and family is who loves you back regardless of blood.

5. **It's A Reason to Put on That Little Black Dress and Rock It** – Go back to your 22 year old self or heck, even your 6 year old self where dressing up was the best thing in the world. You strut a little bit more when you look good. Hell, the mirror is your best friend as you walk down that runway. You are a sexy women! You hold your head a little higher when you look good. You feel more confident when you look good. You remember the strong woman that you are when you look good. You are a Rock Star when you feel good!

> ## C IS FOR CRUSH
> ### NEW WORLD TERM FOR ANNUAL GRAPE HARVEST. REFERS TO BREAKING THE DESTEMMED GRAPE SKINS BEFORE PRESSING AND FERMENTATION.

Here's a breakdown of what a typical Girls Night Out looks like by age:

Twenty Something – Short dresses, high heels, dancing into the night; hot men to your left, hot men to your right. You're young and beautiful and the world is at your fingertips. You're hanging at the local nightclubs where drinks are cheap and the music is loud.

Thirty Something – Young kids, husbands, you still got it so you flaunt it. You just need a night off from the daily grind once in a while to forget adulthood now and then. You're still hitting up happy hours, but it's more of a yuppie crowd. No longer do you need the $2 beers or $2 wells, although it's fun to know you still can hang with those twenty somethings.

Forty Something – Kids are getting older, so they're not attached at the hips anymore. Husbands are getting older…why do they age so nicely? You're feeling more confident than you did in your twenties because you're free to be you. You're more about the time with the gals over drinks, but still ready to party hard when the moment presents itself. And, you can afford the good wines now!

Fifty Plus Something – Dresses, jeans, you don't really give a crap. It's more about who you are with than what you are doing. Your kids are raised, you're enjoying life on your own terms. Luckily, that includes time with the gals and cocktails, always room for cocktails.

"OH YOU'RE ONE OF THOSE." SHAKING HER HEAD SHE POURED THE WINE. "ONE OF THOSE WHAT?" "ONE OF THOSE PEOPLE WHO DRINK ONE GLASS OF RED WINE A NIGHT BECAUSE IT'S HEALTHY, NOT BECAUSE IT TASTE GOOD AND MAKES YOU FEEL LIKE YOU CAN GET TRHOUGH ANOTHER DAY WITHOUT HITTING SOMEONE WITH A FRYNG PAN."
MELANIE HARLOW

YOU'RE CHALLENGE: Plan a Girl's Night Out within the next month or check out our event calendar on our website and join us at your local GGG Chapter to connect with other likeminded women. Just do it and don't keep putting these nights off. Start planning today below!

_____
_____
_____
_____
_____

The Cabernet Sauvignon Girlfriend

Big and Bold flavors are what come to mind when sipping Cabernet Sauvignon. The older the Cabernet Sauvignon, usually the better the wine. Aging lets the flavors really speak volumes to the depth of the wine. As it develops, the wine takes on nuances over time and keeps developing into better experiences. Much like my dearest and oldest friends! We experienced great adventures in our early days of friendship that just keep getting better over the years. These are the friends you may not see every day, but when you are together, it's like you never spent a day a part. You just pick right up and run with the sips! Celebrities I believe to be Cabernet Sauvignon gals…Jennifer Aniston, Amanda Seyfried, Julia Louis-Dreyfus or classics like Maureen O'Hara and Lauren Bacall.

3 Key Inspirations from These Girlfriends:

- Loyalty is priceless in its true form! These gals help you understand fully what loyalty is because they don't run when times are tough. They stand by your side and have your back always.

- Differences aren't what make or break friendships; its how you choose to respect one another's differences! They help you see that it's okay to be different and be friends. A variety of friends is a gift.

- You don't always need to understand everything to be a part of something! You're connected for reasons that others might not understand, but you do and that's what matters.

My Cabernet Sauvignon friends tend to have big and bold personalities, which is why I'm drawn to them. We may not always see eye to eye on everything, but they challenge me to think outside the box. They challenge me to grow in the area of acceptance. They challenge the norm that you have to have everything in common to remain friends for a long time. They're the girlfriends that you may not see regularly as life took you down different highways, but they're the ones who will jump in their cars with a can of frosting and two spoons at a moment's notice in times of need.

These are the friends that held your hair back as you puked into the toilet when you turned 21, and the ones who you'll retire to the coast of Italy with in your old age when husbands have passed, because face it, women outlive men in most cases and what better than to sit on a beach, gray haired with your best friend laughing at the times you were the two gals strutting yourselves around for the boys' attention. Cabernet Sauvignons are those friends that know the good, the bad, the ugly, the pretty, the ones that while it may not make sense to some why you call them friend, it would make even less sense to not still have them in your life.

> **"IF YOUR ARTERIES ARE GOOD, EAT MORE ICE CREAM. IF THEY ARE BAD, DRINK MORE RED WINE. PROCEED THUSLY.**
> **SANDRA BYRD**

Liz is my Cabernet Sauvignon. An unexpected, forced roommate from college that turned into a lifetime of laughter and tears. She's the brunette to my blonde, the one who knows the story behind the carrot woman (I might share that with you one day, but let's just say men seem to like to watch women eat) and the gal I couldn't imagine not being friends with. But, we didn't start that way. Our beginning was my coming home after a class or work, it's been so long…and finding Liz unpacking her belongings into my roommate's room. She popped her head out and said "Hey roomie, I'm just about done." I had no clue what the heck she was talking about. Turns out my other roomie had decided to move out without a word, but figured if she'd found another roommate to cover the bills, it wouldn't be a big deal.

Now, I did know Liz. She was the third of our threesome, but I wasn't exactly thrilled by her. She was nice, but I didn't think we had much in common other than hanging out at the same fraternity house that we were little sisters at. Suddenly, she was constantly with my other Girlfriend and myself and honestly, sometimes drove me a bit nuts….

I thought I'd already found the Louise to my Thelma before Liz. But, bills needed to be paid and I didn't have much of a choice. Or at least that's what I felt at the time. It didn't take long for this big and bold personality to become my true Louise. I owe a lifetime of friendship to that "other" roommate. She did me the biggest favor when she moved Liz in! We've seen each other through loves, divorces, good times and bad. We've lived near and far of each other, and while we're definitely different women these days, we're still Robin and Liz.

Pam is another Cabernet Sauvignon girlfriend of mine. We grew up very differently, but bonded over a few important connections. Sometimes we're talking daily, others not so much, but whenever we are together or talking we pick up right where we left off. That was never more evident than when I flew back during winter to move her cross country back to Colorado from New York. It was several years ago when blizzards were shutting everything down, but somehow, the skies opened up for our five day adventure cross country. I flew in to help pack the moving pod with no flight delays and then drove us back with cassie the pup. We covered a lot of mileage and years over those long daily drives, but you never would have guessed it'd been almost 15 years since we'd last seen each other in person. There was never a quiet moment in those ten hour days. Yes, ten hours of talking sounds like a lot, but the days just flew by for us. I know you gals understand what I'm talking about. In fact, I think sleep was the only thing slowing down our conversations on that road trip. We laughed, we cried and we giggled as we drove cross country. It was one of the most memorable road trips I've had in years. It was just us and the road. A girl's trip for the books.

B IS FOR BRIX
THE SCALE USED TO MEASURE THE SUGAR LEVEL OF THE GRAPE JUICE BEFORE IT'S MADE INTO WINE. THIS ULTIMATELY DETERINES HOW MUCH ALCOHOL A WINE WILL HAVE. EACH GRAM OF SUGAR THAT'S FERMENTED TURNS INTO ABOUT A 1/2 GRAM OF ALCOHOL.

YOUR CHALLENGE: Name 3 of your Cabernet Sauvignon Girlfriends right off the top of your head. Email us their names at info@girlsgonegrape.com and one word that describes them and we'll add you to our monthly emails along with entering you to win a GGG Girlfriends Night In basket! Be sure to tell us they're your Cabernet Sauvignon GF's!

List them here and what they've brought into your life:

_____

_____

_____

P IS FOR PLONK
BRITISH SLANG FOR INEXPENSIVE WINE; ALSO USED TO DESCRIBE LOWER QUALITY WINES.

Girlfriends Annual Trip

Do you remember that night with your girlfriends, as college was coming to an end, when you swore you'd all connect once a year regardless of where you were to celebrate your friendships?

You'd do girl trips, then trips with the hubbies and then the families…There would never be anything that would keep you girls apart long term! Kudos to those of you who actually make this an annual tradition. While most of us had good intentions, life got in the way. Spouses didn't get along with each other or you (Really? How dare them! Didn't they read the clause that says they get you in the deal too?), some had kids/some didn't (damn those different paths down different roads) location, location, location….

Why doesn't anyone tell you that being an adult can get in the way. And, where do we come up with the notion that we can blend our lives so easily? Could it be those lifetime movies? Oh, wait.., most of those are about cheating or murdering husbands…Maybe those should be a clue that it won't be so easy to blend our lives in the next stage!

Liz and I are those friends. We had rose colored glasses on about how wonderfully easy it was going to be to do a girls trip yearly. Of course, we'd love each other's spouses and the spouses would get along. That was never in doubt! Our children would grow up knowing one another and heck, maybe make us true family one day. That's not unreasonable to believe, right? How many of you married your parent's friend's kids? Blah, blah, blah…hello real world! It seems pretty silly now because life did take us in very different directions and while we've spent years on the phone and visited each other, we've actually only done 2 true girlfriend trips. We took a girls weekend trip when my daughter was young and stayed at the Stanley Hotel in Estes Park where we did hair, nails and girly stuff.

The other was an unexpected trip to Guadalajara, Mexico to celebrate our thirtieth birthdays together. Liz and her mother were pretty fluent in Spanish….me, not so much. The three years in junior high school didn't do me very well. Let's just say I learned not to go to another country without at least a basic understanding of the language. Marriage proposals were made and accepted unknowingly. Who knew while hanging at the pool and sipping margaritas, that they weren't asking if I wanted more margaritas? Although, I did get one of the best haircuts I've ever gotten with a spur of the "my hairs driving me crazy so why not get it cut in a foreign country" moment. I had a picture and pointed between the photo and my head and said a lot of "Si". Again, Liz is fluent, but of course, I couldn't wait for her for that adventure. Both trips were fun, but when you realize how long we've been friends and that it's only included these two girlfriend trips, then it becomes rather sad. So, don't discover years down the road that you've spent little time with those girlfriends. They don't need to be long trips. If life makes is so you can't take a trip somewhere, then get together locally for a couple days – maybe to attend events like a wine festival where you go and spend the night together in a hotel. Just be sure to give your relationships the time vested. Invest in those you value and see the returns in how you feel about yourself and those around you. Spending time with your girlfriends is one of the best ways to show yourself a bit of self-care. Of note, I no longer go without making a point of taking some weekends away with the gals.

> "I SHALL DRINK NO WINE BEFORE
> IT'S TIME! OK, IT'S TIME..."
> GROUCHO MARX

Girlfriends are those life jackets in life. They're there for a purpose and while they may not always be needed, it's sure nice to know they're there when the time comes. I'd forgotten how nice it is to just hang with the girls for a few hours laughing and chatting until Girls Gone Grape. I suddenly had girl time available regularly and I couldn't believe how much I had been missing out on.

Spending time with the girls refreshes your soul. Rather you call it sisterhood or girl time, there is something about hanging out with other women that just feeds your spirit.

It's an unspoken connection among women that can't be replaced simply by children, husbands and family. I've had more fun over the past five years and have made some of the dearest friends over sips. Gals I might not have ever met if it wasn't for my husband encouraging me to start my own meetup group looking to meet women who enjoyed wine as much as I did. I now have friends of all different walks in this life. Some are single, some married, some with kids, some without, some adventurers who spark my interests and some that challenge my thoughts. Some have come and gone, but I've loved every minute over the past years.

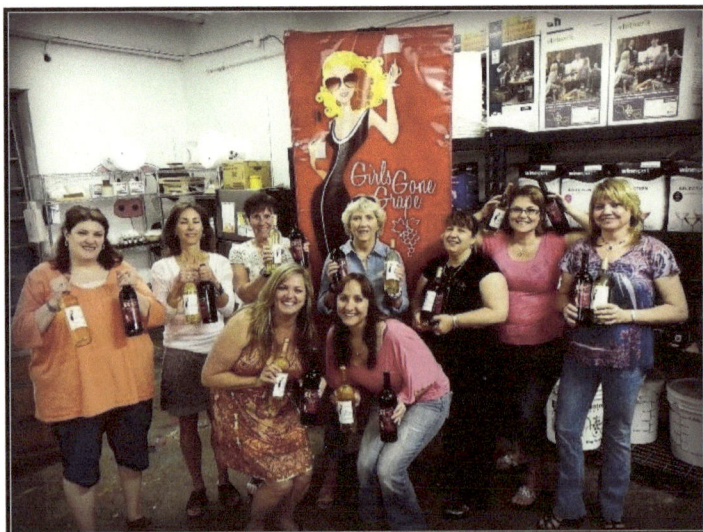

YOUR CHALLENGE: To plan an annual girlfriend's trip with your closest gal pals. It's important to fuel and nourish your soul and what better way than with some girlfriend time! Maybe it's just a quick casual weekend, perhaps it's an adventure of a lifetime type of trip... Maybe it can't be every year, then plan it for every other year, but just plan it.

Use our trip planner on the next page to get started and email us at info@girlsgonegrape.com with a photo of your ideas on your planner to be entered to win a GGG Girls Night In basket! If you find yourself stuck in the what-to-do phase, you can always check out our Girls Gone Grape Travel Group and join in our annual adventure! At the start of this book we were planning our first Girl's Weekend Get-A-Way in Vail, Colorado for an "I Love Lucy" style Grape Stomp where we danced in grape buckets under the Rocky Mountains and took on the mountains in Jeeps laughing till we were full of wine and sass. During the debut of this book we will be immersed in our villa near the towns of Tuscany, Italy immersing ourselves in culture, food and wine. Check out where we're going next over at www.girlsgonegrape.com under our GGG Travel Group Page in our events section. Heck, we may plan several get-a-ways a year!

> "WHEN I OPENED UP THE BOTTLE OF WINE, THEBES SAID WHOA, YOU YANKED THAT CORK OUT LIKE YOU WERE SAVING IT FROM DROWNING. SHE GOT OUT HER MARKERS AND DREW A SCREAMING FACE ON THE CORK."
> MIRIAM TOEWS

GIRLFRIEND'S TRIP PLANNER

DATE: _____

LOCATION: _____

WHOSE INVITED:
_____
_____
_____

ADVENTURES:
_____
_____
_____

BUDGET: _____

RESERVATIONS MADE:
_____
_____
_____
_____
_____
_____

SALUTE! YOU'RE ON YOUR WAY TO A FABULOUS TRIP WITH YOUR WINE CLUB GALS!

The Sauvignon Blanc Girlfriend

Well balanced with witty characteristics is what pops to mind when thinking of a good New Zealand Sauvignon Blanc. It's crisp, fruity and versatile. It's a knock your socks off kind of wine that can turn anything into a story. Its unique characteristics make it stand out. Some are citrusy, tropical, or even grassy – it's a wine that takes on its own personality and shouts "take me as I am or spit me out….I'm okay either way." This wine can stand on its own or play nicely with others, just like my Sauvignon Blanc girlfriends. Celebrities that come to mind as Sauvignon Blanc gals are Drew Barrymore, Amy Schumer, Melissa McCarthy or classics like Lucille Ball or Mae West.

3 Key Inspirations from These Girlfriends:

- You'll be okay laughing at yourself. These friends are confident enough in themselves that laughing at themselves is second nature.

- To love yourself just as you are. You learn to not get caught up in the hype of who people think you should be because these friends show you how to be comfortable in your own skin and life.

- Laughter is the best solution for everything. You can't always control the curves that life throws at us, but these friends' help you understand how to find the humor and look for the good in all situations. You ran out of your favorite shampoo right before a date? Did you know you can wash your hair in beer? Bonus, men love the smell of beer!

Humor is a must in our lives and these gals exemplify tickling your funny bones! Witty and unique also describe your Sauvignon Blanc girlfriends. They're the ones that keep you smiling and laughing as you never know what's going to come out of their mouths. One minute they're seriously discussing the events of the day and the next, they're shocking you with their answers in a Cards against Humanity game. They're softer spoken than most, but don't ever be fooled by that quietness. Behind the quietness is a world of wisdom and a heart of loyalty. This is the friend that can stand alone and celebrate her independence, but also knows that all hearts need connection. She's the one who will give you the shirt off her back, the food off her table and only asks in return that you show her the real you. No gimmicks, no show pony rides, just honesty and pure joy is what you'll find in your sauvignon Blanc girlfriends.

H IS FOR HOT
A DESCRIPTION FOR WINE THAT IS HIGH IN ALCOHOL.

Kristie is one of my closest Sauvignon Blanc girlfriends. She's an unexpected delight! Someone I didn't know prior to Girls Gone Grape and may have never run into her without having started GGG. We've spent the last year on weekend adventures travelling from Colorado to Utah, New Mexico, Wyoming and South Dakota! Lots of sips and stories created; some with just the two of us and others with our families. I have had some of the heartiest laughs courtesy of Kristie. She's my pal that shocks everyone at the table during Cards Against Humanity because she certainly is too sweet to have been the one to put THAT card in! She's the pal that knows it's just easier to hand me her car keys wherever we go due to my motion sickness or maybe that's my control sickness? She's the one who is up to trying anything at least once, even if she does end up with bruises all over! She's the gal pal that leaves the best books on her coffee table when I bring my husband over…"How to Murder the Man of Your Dreams," "How to Murder Your Mother In Law." It's her desserts that let her get away with those books! She's the gal pal that has become more family over the years and the member that keeps us smiling!

Eve is Sauvignon Blanc to the letter. She was one of the firsts to become a Champagne member when we opened up membership to Girls Gone Grape. She's the one that had us in stitches at every event as she'd have no problem walking up to another table in the restaurant to tell a gal her husband had the best handlebar mustache she'd ever seen. She's the first to jump into the dance line around the Greek restaurant and the one to put the first hole in the kitchen wall while shouting "OOMPA". In her defense, it was the owner that gave us the plates and encouraged us all to throw them into his wall and shatter them. Hey, he was Greek…enough said. Her laughter is contagious. Her spirit is joyful.

"WHEN WINE ENTERS, OUT GOES THE TRUTH."
BEN FRANKLIN

YOU'RE CHALLENGE: Name 3 of your Sauvignon Blanc Girlfriends right off the top of your head. Email us their names at info@girlsgonegrape.com and one word that describes them and we'll add you to our monthly drawing to you to win a GGG Girlfriends Night In basket! Be sure to tell us they're your Sauvignon Blanc GF's!   List them here and what they've brought   into   your   life:

_____

_____

_____

_____

_____

_____

Chocolate & Wine

Chocolate and wine are two of my vices! I WILL NOT give either of them up! I will spend more time in the gym in order to keep these vices! Luckily, according to Author/Chocolatier Julie Pech of The Chocolate Therapist, the right type of chocolate daily can actually keep you healthy! She eats chocolate daily and looks awesome! Julie is the reason for this chapter because after attending several of her classes on Chocolate & Wine Pairing, I'm not able to look at chocolate the same.

Once you learn how to taste chocolate the right way, then throw in wine, you're going to start having more orgasmic experiences that might rival the ones in bed! Not to give our lovers the short end of the stick, so to speak, but......chocolate and wine is just plain sexy!

I'm not talking the candy bar off the shelf at the gas station chocolate, gals. I'm talking the premium, handmade chocolates that you'll find in the shops in your neighborhood made by people who are passionate about chocolate. There is a difference! I'm telling you from firsthand experience, that if you spend a little more on your chocolate, you'll see the benefits and not need as much chocolate to curb your craving.

But, I want to stay on chocolate and wine, so I encourage you to order Julie Pech's books (www.thechocolatetherapist.com) if you want to really understand chocolate! I'm going to give you 5 quick tips on hosting your own chocolate & wine tasting that will leave your friends wanting more...or maybe their lovers asking you "what the hell did you give to my sweetie?"

Tip 1 – You only need a little nibble of a good chocolate. Don't stuff the whole piece of chocolate in your mouth. You may be tempted, but slow down and read the next step.

Tip 2 – You need to let it melt in your mouth, rather than chomp it down. Think of sipping a glass of wine! You don't chug your wine (unless of course, you're playing our Sip It or Spill It game and draw the chug your wine card. You sip and savor! Do the same with your chocolate. Julie paired 5 chocolates pieces with 5 wines and I was worried it wouldn't be enough, but I actually took chocolate home with me as my senses were on overload. It was orgasmic!

Tip 3 – Just as the chocolate is on the verge of being gone, take a sip of the wine you've chosen to pair with it. Notice the hints of chocolate as they mingle with the wine. What are you picking up? Is the wine more powerful or is the chocolate? Did they blend perfectly together?

Tip 4 – Be adventurous in your pairings; don't just use basic dark or light chocolate. Try infusing things by using out of the norm chocolates; red chili pepper dark chocolate or apricot milk chocolates. The more unique the chocolate offerings, the more unique the tasting.

Tip 5 – Dark chocolates tend to do better with red wines while lighter, milk chocolates pair nicely with white wine. That said, don't be afraid to mix things up as everyone's taste are different and you might just find a new favorite in a combo you never would have imagined!

YOU'RE CHALLENGE: Plan a chocolate & wine tasting with your girlfriends! Everyone brings a bottle of wine, but assign them each a different type, so you can plan your chocolate pairings. Use our suggestions on the next page based on our wine pack girlfriends! Most of the suggestions are from my tasting at The Chocolate Therapist, plus a few of my own. Email us a photo of your pack enjoying the night at info@girlsgonegrape.com to be entered to win a GGG Girls Night In basket! Be sure to send us a photo of the wines and chocolate you chose to pair. We'll share them on our social media platforms giving your pack the credit for the combos!

Chocolate & Wine suggestions for your Wine Pack of GF's!

CHAMPAGNE - FRESH STRAWBERRIES DIPPED IN WHITE CHOCOLATE OR APPLE PIE WITH MELTED MILK CHOCOLATE & COCONUT FLAKES

SAUVIGNON BLANC - FRESH PEAR DIPPED IN MELTED MILK CHOCOLATE INFUSED WITH GROUND NUTMEG OR MILK CHOCOLATE INFUSED WITH AMARETTO

ROSE - WHITE CHOCOLATE COVERED MACADAMIA NUTS OR FRESH STRAWBERRIES DIPPED IN MILK CHOCOLATE

SHIRAZ - DARK CHOCOLATE CAYENNE PEPPER CHOCOLATES OR DARK CHOCOLATE CARAMELS TOPPED WITH CHILI PEPPER POWDER

CABERNET SAUVIGNON - CHOCOLATE CHIP OATMEAL COOKIES DIPPED IN MELTED DARK CHOCOLATE OR DARK CHOCOLATE MINTS

MOST OF THESE PAIRINGS ARE THINGS I'VE TRIED AFTER READING JULIE PECH'S BOOK "DARE TO PAIR." YOU COULD ALSO VISIT WWW.THECHOCOLATETHERAPIST.COM AND PICK UP HER EXCLUSIVE DARK CHOCOLATE AND MILK CHOCOLATE COLLECTIONS WITH SUGGESTED WINE PAIRINGS TO MAKE LIFE EASY!

The Rosé Girlfriend

There is a season for every Rosé. It's rather short, but it can pack some delightful notes. And because it's seasonal, its flavors can change from year to year determined by Mother Nature. Some years are off, some years are full of flavor. Rosés tend to be light with tones of pale to bright pinks and fruity. This wine sort of flows in and out of our wine preference. Some Rosé's will leave a bad taste while others tickle your spirit, but it's always new and exciting with each passing season to discover the nuances of a good Rosé. That's how to describe my girlfriends that fall into the Rosé category. Delightful at the moment, but just meant for the moment. Celebrities that make me think of Rosé are Lisa Kudrow, Brooke Shields, Demi Moore or classics like Bette Davis or Natalie Wood. (Note: these gals more for characters they've played through the years)

3 Key Inspirations from These Girlfriends:

- Not everything lasts forever, but that doesn't make it any less valuable to your heart! Be in that moment for however long it is.

- Some of the loudest life lessons are taught in short spans! We're always learning, but don't discredit the short lessons.

- Your instincts will lead you to what is best for you at the right times in your life! You need a challenge… life is going to give you one. You need a break…life is going to give you one. Things happen when they're supposed to.

Your Rosé friends are those friends that appear at the right moment in life providing what your soul needs at that point in time. There is a distinct reason for the friendship. A season for it to bloom and share bounty in, but as each season comes to an end, so is typical of this friendship. These aren't always our longest friendships, but they aren't ones to mourn. Rather, they should be celebrated as these friendships bring so many lessons into our lives. Sometimes they're lessons we want and sometimes lessons we need even if we didn't want them. These friendships really help you tune into your feelings and instincts.

I find that as women we sometimes question our instincts because of what everyone around us is saying or doing. I've found my Rosé friends have really helped me to understand that it's okay to listen to that little voice in my head. I've had some challenging Rosé friendships over the years. Yes, a few I would call just plain ugly. Yet, even in those friendships, I learned valuable lessons. Lessons that make us stronger women.

N IS FOR NOSE
TERM USED TO DESCRIBE THE
BOUQUET AND AROMA OF THE WINE.

Marcia was my childhood best friend who I swung on the playground swings with in elementary school. She lived down the street and we became inseparable. She knew about my first crush on the newspaper boy Doug. She shared in my first tears as he "dated" someone else in our class. Then middle school came and her family moved away. In my senior year of high school I was introduced to a friend of a friend that went to another high school that turned out to be Marcia. She was back in my life like a force of nature. I wasn't very confident during my senior year of high school. Marcia, on the other hand was confident to an extreme.

She'd walk into a room and steam roll over all the guys. The more we started doing things together, the more I started coming out of this shell of self-doubt. I felt prettier hanging out with her. The boys seemed to notice me more when I was out with her. I stopped letting my father's negative remarks about everything I did make or break me. I was experiencing things (some good, some bad) that I might have never experienced if it hadn't been for Marcia dragging me along. We became little sisters to one of the local fraternities in college, we spent spring break in Dallas. Marcia is the girlfriend that taught me how to lighten up and stop doubting my every move. She was my best friend. I trusted her like no other.

After a few years she moved to Dallas and I was going to join her until some truths starting popping up that made me see things about that friendship in a different light. The friendship ended badly. But, Marcia gave me several lifetime gifts during our years together. She taught me to keep my eyes more open to my girlfriends around me and not blindly believe in their friendships over all others. She was the girl that helped me find my flirty, sexy self-confidence. She brought Liz into my life. For those gifts, I can say I will never regret our friendship even though it soured. I did look her up in my early 40's, as Facebook makes it very easy to find old pals. I discovered she'd passed away. It was a loss I felt more deeply than I would have thought based on the ending of that friendship, but again, it was the loss of someone who played a valuable role in my life.

Then there was Jessica in my thirties. A woman I met through networking events who was driven, ambitious, fun, and crazy and had a daughter the same age as mine. She lived a life out loud when I met her and I was drawn to her energy. She believed in me as I embarked on a career path that sort of fell in my lap. We became inseparable and as I navigated the paths of a divorce, and then new love, she was there including my daughter and I in her family's lives. My apartment was too small for hosting birthday parties, but Jessica opened her home for my daughter's parties. We'd shop, we'd sip, we'd laugh, we'd cry. We supported one another and were each other's cheerleaders for a time. We traveled the road together for a while and then it was time for us to head in different directions.

> # O IS FOR OAKY
> TERM USED TO DESCRIBE A WINE THAT PRESENTS FLAVORS AND CHARACTERISTICS IMPARTED BY OAK AGING. TYPES OF OAK USED VARY(BARREL, SHIPS, TOASTED, AMERICAN, FRENCH) AND CAN RANGE FROM VANILLA TO SMOKY FLAVORS.

We reconnected several years later and it was sweet to catch up with where life had taken us and our children. Yet again, we'd become different women, so a new season never really took place. And that's okay, because again, I took lessons from this friendship that are priceless. I tried new things with her that I might not have tried. I discovered how women working together to build each other up can accomplish amazing things when they set their minds to it. I learned that it's okay to ask for help through this friendship. And I learned to go with my instincts even when others may not agree with you because you are the one that decides who or what is right for you. If I'd listened to her, rather than myself, I wouldn't be going on twenty years with my best friend today. I will forever be grateful for the friendship of Jessica.

In recent years, there have been many Rosé friendships that have come and gone. Some have moved, others were just lessons for a moment, but all women I wouldn't trade those moments with for anything. They taught me lessons of good and bad, silly and sad, but all lessons that continue to make me the woman I am today and will be tomorrow.

Rosé girlfriends are vital friendships that we all need to have. They aren't meant to necessarily be long term ones, but they are meant to teach you something you need at that time in your life. Maybe it's a major lesson, maybe a little one, but each and every petal of those rosé gals is worth every single moment you spent or will spend with them.

YOU'RE CHALLENGE: Name 3 of your Rosé Girlfriends right off the top of your head. Email us their names at info@girlsgonegrape.com and one word that describes them and we'll add you to our monthly drawings to win a GGG Girlfriends Night In basket! Be sure to tell us they're your Rosé GF's! List them here and what they've brought into your life:

_____

_____

_____

_____

_____

The Ultimate Mimosa Bar Challenge

One of my favorite things to sip on is a fabulous Mimosa on a weekend morning! It's even more fabulous when surrounded by my girlfriends with a spread for creating the ultimate mimosa combinations laid out in front of us to play with! Mimosas are easy to make as you're basically combining champagne with Orange juice. The ratio of the two depends on your preference. I prefer more champagne than orange juice, but it can get a bit silly early on if you're pouring more champagne! Being a bit ticklish never bothers me....but go with your tastes on this one.

While perhaps not considered a true Mimosa, it is fun to get creative with other juices and goodies! Try mixing Champagne with Peach nectar. The Italians call this a Bellini! Whether you use Champagne, Prosecco, or Cava, it's all about the bubbles to get started! And because you're mixing, you needn't purchase the most expensive type to create a fabulous mimosa or Bellini!

Note: Champagne is from the Champagne region of France, but other sparklers from other regions in France will work just as nicely. Prosecco is sparkling wine from Italy. Cava is sparkling wine from Spain. You're not supposed to call it all Champagne, so bubbly and sparkling are other names you'll hear. And, don't forget the sparklers from the USA and other New World Regions. For instance, there is a fun sparkling rose out of New Zealand called Sophora Sparkling Rose that is a fun spin on a mimosa. Prosecco tends to make for a sweeter Mimosa, while Champagne and Cava tend to make a drier mimosa. Just a few things to keep in mind or help you understand why not all bubbles are called Champagne. There is legal jargon protecting the Champagne region, but do you really need to know all that....I think not. So, grab a flute and get pouring those bubbles!

Then you throw in some pretties like flowers, linen or things that make you feel wonderful and invite your gal pals over. Maybe have a theme for the day like spending the day in Greece by having a movie marathon watching the movie Mama Mia. Drink Greek wines, yes there are Greek wines to sip on. Or, maybe it's more of a gal pal day with movies like Thelma & Louise, Romy & Michelle's High School Reunion, A League of Their Own, and Waiting to Exhale.

Thoughts to get your Mimosa bar started:

JUICES	FRUITS	EXTRAS
Orange Juice	Raspberries	Fresh Mint
Peach Nectar	Strawberries	Ice Buckets
Apricot Nectar	Star Fruit	Chalkboards
Cranberry Juice	Blueberries	Pretty Glasses
Pineapple Juice	Pineapple	Tablecloths/Linens
Pomegranate Juice	Peaches	Flowers
Grapefruit Juice	Apricots	Basil, fresh herbs

A few favorites I use regularly for my Mimosa's are:

La Marca Prosecco– This lends to a sweeter mimosa.

Cavicchioli 1928 Prosecco – Extra Dry (1928 is the year they became a winery, not the year of the Prosecco. I always get asked that, so thought I'd clear that up first thing). Not into sweet, then this is a good one for mixing with juice.

The Shiraz Girlfriend

Spicy, sassy and ever so classy! If you've had a good Shiraz, then you know exactly what I'm talking about and at this very moment, you're also picturing those friends of yours that fit this description to the letter! A good Shiraz has just enough hints of spice to leave your taste buds tingling while being balanced enough to still be a smooth sip going down. It should leave you wanting for more. Those who enjoy Shiraz tend to be looking for something with a little kick on the end, something that is a bit spicy, grab your attention and not ordinary. Shiraz isn't a safe sip like a Pinot Noir with a light and sensible pour, but more of a pour that challenges you. Celebrities that come to mind for me as Shiraz gals are Angelina Jolie, Goldie Hawn, Kate Hudson and Susan Sarandon.

3 Key Inspirations from These Girlfriends:

- They inspire you to want to find your creative outlets. We all have a creative streak, it's just a matter of finding out what yours is.

- Sassy and classy go hand in hand! You don't have to be one or the other. They play nicely together.

- Dream! Then find a way to make that dream your reality! They inspire you to seek out what you want to create in this life and help you find the courage to go after it.

Your Shiraz girlfriends are those that have a bit of sass to their class. They are always up for a new challenge. They're the ones that live life by the code that until you've tried something at least once, how can you know whether or not you like it. They travel or dream of traveling to locales and immersing themselves in the culture around them. You tell them they can't do something and they go out and find a way to do it.

She's the girlfriend that has a bit of Audrey Hepburn, Lucille Ball and Angelina Jolie in her genes. She's stylish whether in a t-shirt and jeans or dolled up for a cocktail party and most importantly, she's the friend with that look.....you know the look, hell maybe sometimes you're the shiraz in your circle. It's a glimmer in the eyes, followed by a smirk of a smile that tells you she's up to something. She's extremely creative and tends to be the artist of your group.

A IS FOR AOC
ABBREVIATION FOR APPELLATION D'ORIGINE CONTROLEE (CONTROLLED DESIGNATION OF ORIGIN), THE AGENCY VIA FRENCH GOVERNMENT THAT CONTROLS AND REGULATES WINE PRODUCTION.

Sherry and Julia fall into my sassy Shiraz girlfriends and I pair them here because I feel like whenever I see one, the other is just over my shoulder. Over the past few years of getting to know them I'm often caught up in the contagious laughter that oozes from them. I've seen them from their dressed to kill looks down to paint on their noses and they always exude class. Julia has traveled the world as a former Airline Attendant turned painter extraordinaire and did I mention, she's British. She's one of my girl crushes just for the accent alone. Sherry's travels have stayed closer to home, but have involved helping others with disabilities. She has such a heart for people and positive attitude regardless of what detours life throws at her and she's had a few doozies. They are two women that will try anything new and do it with smiles! And those glimmering eyes and smirks run rampart with these two and I wouldn't have them any other way.

Julia's the artist/creator of the two. She can turn the ordinary into the extraordinary, whether she's using a paintbrush or putting together a girls night in basket. She's free spirited, might be the English in her and draws you in with her quirky wit. Sherry has a heart of gold and it shows in the way she interacts with her friends and family. She jumps in with everything she has and then figures things out as she goes. Lots of fun sips shared with these Shiraz gals. These two are proof that Shiraz characteristics can vary based on the terroir, but it's always fun sipping a Shiraz regardless of locale with a Shiraz girlfriend.

Y IS FOR YIELD
MEASURE OF THE AMOUNT OF GRAPES OR WINE THAT IS PRODUCED PER UNIT SURFACE OF VINEYARD. USUALLY IN TONS PER ACRE.

YOU'RE CHALLENGE: Name 3 of your Shiraz Girlfriends right off the top of your head. Email us their names at info@girlsgonegrape.com and one word that describes them and we'll add you to our monthly emails along with entering you to win GGG Girlfriends Night In basket! Be sure to tell us they're your Shiraz GF's!

List them here and what they've brought into your life:

_____
_____
_____
_____
_____
_____
_____
_____
_____
_____

See. Swirl. Smell. Sip. Savor

The 5 S's associated with proper wine tasting! Do you ever just want to say "DUH..." to the Wine Pro as they explain those S's, like we're in elementary school and have no clue what we're doing? I mean is it really that hard to sip a glass of wine? NO! It isn't. Here's my take on those damn 5 steps...

SEE – Of course I'm looking at what I'm sipping! Who the hell doesn't check what they're sipping before they put that glass to their lips! Hello...I don't want to put someone else's lip stained glass to my lips! If it's red wine, its shades of red from light to dark. If it's white wine, its shades of pale to yellow from light to dark. If it's blue wine, a new craze apparently, you're on your own as who knows what the hell is up with blue wine! Boom, I see what I'm drinking!

Serious note: if you look, really look at that wine in your glass, you can get a pretty good idea of its age and body. Lighter colored wines tend to be younger and lighter on the sip. The darker the wine, the older and typically fuller the wine on the sips. There are shades in all red and white wines if you look close enough.

SWIRL – Let's be honest....you hate the person to your left that has the prettiest swirl around. Damn it, how do they make it look so easy! Then they tell you "to get started, put your glass on a table and swirl it around gently that way until you get better." Screw that! I say, swirl to your heart's content! Maybe a bit spills out of your glass...so, lick it up! Ok, that might not be lady like, so tap it with your fingers and then suck on your fingers...hey, it's cute when babies do it!

Serious note: I think you should actually smell the wine first, then swirl it and smell again. Swirling actually opens up the wine in your glass and gives it a chance to dance with the oxygen and give you a few extra hints about what's going to hit your mouth.

SMELL - It's not polite to crack up at the gal next to you who has her nose buried in the glass. Her nose isn't that big, really, it's the glass enhancing the appearance of her nose! And there is a reason the guy has his mouth and nose in the glass at the same time even though it looks like he's hyperventilating…

Serious note: I love to smell my wines and let my personal Sherlock Holmes get her deduction on! My favorite way, which I think is more subtle and I believe gives you a broader sense is to take my glass to my nose slightly tilted and roll the glass from the side to the front of my nose to pick up notes. Then at the very end, I'll inhale the aromas with my mouth slightly open to see what tastes pop to mind. Yes, you have permission to laugh at me if you like, but first you have to realize what I'm doing!

> **"I LIKE ON THE TABLE, WHEN WE'RE SPEAKING, THE LIGHT OF A BOTTLE OF INTELLIGENT WINE."**
> **PABLO NERUDA**

SIP – Not some sissy little sip. Not some huge chug, but a good size sip to play around in your mouth with. Don't go being coy on me now, you know darn well what playing around in your mouth size is good for you! And, no need to turn red as you're most likely reading this book solo anyhow!

Serious note: You want enough of a sip to swirl from front to back and side to side to give yourself a chance to really dance with this sip. The sweet notes are going to be at the tip of your tongue, while the dryer notes and acidity are going to be felt more in your cheeks and going down your throat.

SAVOR – The afterglow of that orgasmic sex you just had! Oh, wait…we're talking wine! But, just like chocolate, sometimes wine can be more pleasurable than sex!

Serious note: Savoring that first sip by not automatically sipping another gives your Sherlock Holmes a chance to determine how right the clues were. Does the wine taste like what the aroma suggested? Or, does the after note leave new flavors for you to ponder? Enjoy that sip for a moment. This is the true moment you discover if you love, like or dislike this wine. Because after you keep sipping, your senses get a bit tingly and it all starts tasting the same.

See. Swirl. Smell. Sip. Savor! Throw out the rules and just enjoy the moment! It doesn't really matter how you sip your wine, just as long as you're sipping more wine!

Robin Salls

SEE

SWIRL

SMELL

SIP

SAVOR

Girls Gone Grape

Girls "Night in" – 5 ideas to connect

While a Girls "Night Out" can be a lot of fun, it can potentially add up to a lot of coin if you're doing them regularly. And remember, we've already been over the reasons why you can't live without Girls Night out, so we don't want to send you mixed signals. On that note, we want to suggest that some of those girls' nights fall into "Night's in". It's amazing just how much fun can be had behind closed doors (not the bedroom ones) when you're not worried about driving or public consumption! You can get really creative at home! Hell, you could even channel your 16 year old self and have a good ole fashion sleepover! Be crazy, drink fabulous sips, turn the music up and dance! Here's 5 thoughts to get your juices going....

Sugar/Salt Scrubs & Wine - I love to treat my inside to fabulous sips while treating my outside to fabulous scrubs! So much so, that after much exploration and testing of various recipes we finally created one that I love to share at Girls Gone Grape Events! We hold at least one or two a year that bring the gals together to sip and make personalized scrubs to take home. The last one was actually called Sugar Scrubs & Sangria! We sipped on red sangria and white sangria as we filled wonderful jars full of scrubs that leave your skin baby soft. It can get a bit crazy with a room of over 20 plus gals, so it's an ideal girls night in when you gather a few of your closest friends.

I'm going to give you the GGG recipe right now. The ingredients call out to my Italian roots, along with nurturing my skin in the dry, Colorado weather (GGG is headquartered in Colorado), so you may have to play with the recipe a bit to find the ideal scrub for your skin and your location, but it's a fabulous starting point and it's all natural ingredients that are easy to find!

Sugar Scrub Recipe:
- 2 Cups White Sugar
- 1 Large Scoop Epsom Salts (about ¼ cup or shot glass size, when I say scoop)
- 2 Large Scoops Pink Himalayan Salt
- 2 Large Scoops Dead Sea Salt
- 2 Squirts Vitamin E Oil
- 1 ¾ Cups Pure Extra Virgin Olive Oil (Coconut Oil or Grapeseed Oil could be substituted)
- Natural Oil drops in various scents (I love using tangerine oil drops as it wakes me up and refreshes me. I've also used peppermint drops and thrown in Cocoa powder for holiday scrubs) Use as many drops as needed to get the scent you love.

Mix the sugar and salts together, then add the vitamin E oil. Add in enough Olive Oil to create an applesauce consistency. Then add your scent and mix. Scoop into pint size jars. This recipe creates about 2 pint jars. I like to use the old fashion glass jars for appearance, but any jar will due. Create a fun label to slap on your jar! I've even been known to throw a bit of red wine or champagne in for a decadent scrub.

> "WINE IS BOTTLED POETRY"
> ROBERT LOUIS STEVENSON

Sip It or Spill It Game Night – I noticed at some of our events we needed something to kick start the night. I love games, so I decided to combine a Truth or Dare and Spin the Bottle type game together. Viola, Sip It or Spill It became the GGG ice breaker game. You spin a mini Champagne bottle filled with sand around the GGG gal board ending on either Sip It or Spill it. Then you take the matching card piece and follow the instruction. Sip it cards are basically the dare cards in our game. Things like "Chug your wine or Take a sip while doing your best yoga move" will get you up and moving around. Spill it cards are basically your truth cards; "Who's your celebrity crush or tell us who your hottest friend on Facebook is". Request your free printable game over at info@girlsgonegrape.com or head to the shop to get the extended version of our game.

> "I COOK WITH WINE, SOMETIMES I
> EVEN ADD IT TO THE FOOD."
> W.C. FIELDS

Limoncello Cocktails – I love limoncello! It can be sipped alone or added to cocktails. We're going to give you several recipes to sip on with your girlfriends. I suggest you put on the movie "Under the Tuscan Sun" and sit back and sip with the gals. The best Limoncellos are the ones from Italy, but you can use whatever you can find in your area. You're going to try sipping the Limoncello by itself and then combining it with Prosecco and Gin.

Limoncello Prosecco Kiss

1 part Limoncello
2 parts Prosecco
2 parts Seltzer water
Sugared Mint Leaves optional (dip leaves in water & sugar, let dry)

Start with a high ball glass. Add limoncello, prosecco and seltzer. Add Sugared Mint leaves and serve.

If you get really ambitious, you can try making your own limoncello. The benefit of making your own is that you can control how sweet or strong your final Limoncello comes out. You should give it a try at least once! I'll even throw in my family recipe for you to give a try. You'll find it in the back of this book. But don't cheat and skip to the back to find it now, as you'll miss out on all the other good stuff to come.

Limoncello Collins

1 part Gin
3/4 part Limoncello
1/4 part Fresh Lemon Juice
Sliced Lemons
3 Parts club soda or seltzer

Start with a shaker of ice, add gin, limoncello and lemon juice. Shake. Fill high ball glass with fresh ice and lemon slices. Pour cocktail and top off with club soda.

The Limoncello Collins is a good drink for those who like something a bit less sweet. Limoncello is a great aperitif or after dinner drink to help with digestion. That's what it was originally used in the early days. Now I sip on it simply because I love it especially on a warm summer day. It's grown up lemonade! Perhaps you could set up a grown up lemonade stand? Hey, there's an idea for a theme in your backyard to share this fabulous Limoncello gals night out!

Can You Guess the Expensive Bottle –?

Invite the girls over having each of them bring a different bottle of wine and tapas to share. Give them a price limit, say under $15. Then pick up a more expensive wine. It's your girls, so splurge a little. While the gals set up the tapas, slip into another room and cover each bottle's label, marking them by numbers including the expensive bottle. Be sure to remove the bottle neck foils if it gives away the wine! After all, you're trying to guess the wines!

Hand out paper and pens to take notes because this is a great way to build your palate and wine sense. (You'll find a tasting note sheet in the back of the book that you can photo copy). Note the flavors you pick up and what your gal pals are sensing. Do you seem to have the same tastes or are you each picking up different flavors? Start tasting the wines in 2 oz. pours, about the size of your thumb. At the end have everyone guess which bottle is the expensive one. Then see what the thoughts are on the rest of the wines.

Cover your bottles as simply as wrapping some pretty paper around the bottle and securing with tape or pick up empty gift bags to put them in. Just be sure you can't see through the cover to the label.

Better yet, pull out your creative side and make your own burlap label covers that can be reusable. Because after tasting like this, you'll want to do it over and over. It's super easy. Here are the steps and you can see a sample in the photo above:

1) Cut strips of burlap long enough to wrap around the bottle with a little overlapping at the ends. You can find burlap at most craft stores and it's fairly inexpensive. In the photo I used an outdoor burlap that has a plastic lining to the back side that gives it more durability, but regular burlap works too.

2) Paint your numbers on and allow to dry. Freehand it or use stencils, but have fun. I feel 5 label wraps for 5 bottles is a good tasting number. It gives you variety, but shouldn't dull your senses if you're pouring it right. Wink! Wink!

3) Purchase self-sticking Velcro, easy to find at craft stores, plus there's no sewing needed. Take one end the burlap and place the softer part of the Velcro on the outside or top of burlap. Measure out the same amount of the joining piece. Then on the inside piece of burlap, add the connecting piece. Make sure the burlap is pulled tightly so, you won't have the labels slipping down too easily.

Presto. A fun way to cover your bottles for this tasting.

Movie Night

Sometimes you just want to hang with the girls and get lost in a good chick flick. The ones that most the guys would rather pull their hair out than sit and watch with you.

Amp your movie night up with choosing a theme for the night. For example, plan an Italian night and choose movies that take place in Italy (Under the Tuscan Sun, Letters to Juliet) and then find wines from the towns the movies were filmed in. Or, teach yourself Italian by watching Italian movies in the Italian Language, like La Dolce Vita. Type in Sophia Loren movies in google and go crazy choosing only the ones filmed in Italian!

Or how about playing around with a movie theme. Take Willy Wonka and the Chocolate Factory (Original or remake as Johnny Depp is easy on the eyes no matter what character he plays). Take each type of candy from the movie and pair it with a wine or cocktail with similarities. Make a blueberry Cosmo for the blueberry scene, just be careful so you don't turn yourself blue!

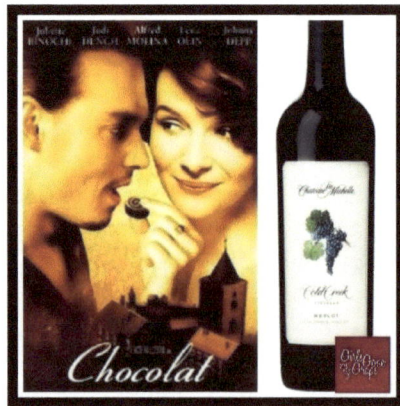

To Sommelier or Not

I told you in the beginning that I am not a Sommelier, rather just a gal who grew up with wine being a vital core part of my lifestyle. My Great Grandfather was a bootlegger during Prohibition in Upstate New York, running wine and booze into New York City. I can still remember the corks bursting from the bottles my parents didn't cork right, upon a cherry wine making adventure in my childhood home. I don't remember a time or dinner where there wasn't a bottle of wine available. Perhaps not available for me personally due to age, but wine has always had a presence in my life of some type.

I've thought of taking the time and money to invest in becoming a Sommelier. Those credentials could look really nice behind my name. But, just as often as I think about doing so, I also wonder if I really need to go in that direction. If you've ever found yourself wondering the same thing, then this chapter might help you decide if becoming a Sommelier is in your future. The first question to ask yourself is why are you interested in becoming a Sommelier?

> **B IS FOR BODY**
> A SENSATION DESCRIBING THE WEIGHT AND FULLNESS OF A WINE IN YOUR MOUTH. A WINE CAN BE LIGHT, MEDIUM OR FULL BODIED.

Do you want a career in the wine business? Do you want to work at a winery or for a wine distributor? Are you looking to work in a high end restaurant? Are you wanting to open a wine shop? If you answered yes, then taking the plunge to become a Sommelier might be right for you.

Do you want to learn more about wine, so you understand what you're ordering? Do you want to impress your boss with your wine knowledge? Are you bored and you like to take courses to earn certificates? If you answered yes, then taking the plunge to become a Sommelier might be right for you.

Do you see a pattern? Only you know if becoming a Sommelier is for you. There is no right or wrong answer to the questions above. I have friends that are winemakers, but not sommeliers. I have friends that are sommeliers, but not winemakers. While those credentials might open a few doors easier, it's not impossible to open the doors without them. There is also the education component to consider too. There are different schools that have different requirements for the certification. For instance The International Wine Guild program is much shorter and easier to pass than the Court of Master Sommeliers. The cost may be a factor in decisions too based the program chosen. Perhaps, watching the movie "Somm" would give you some perspective regarding the path to take and if it's right for you. I think if watching this movie leaves you breathless, rather than frightened, then you might just want to become a Somm. There's a lot more than just a glamourous title involved.

> ## "WHAT CHANCE DOES LOGIC HAVE AGAINST A GLASS OF WINE AND A KISS?"
> ## MARTY RUBIN

The world of wine can be seductive. Especially when you're looking from the outside in. How glamourous it is to spend your days making wine, sipping wine, travelling to vineyards around the world, and attending fabulous events to promote wine. Right?

There is glamour, but almost every Women in Wine that I have met, especially those with the glamourous titles of Winery Owner, Winemaker or Sommelier will tell you that while they love living their passion, it is not as glamourous as the world paints it. Know your reasons for why you're thinking of becoming a Sommelier and listen to your instinct. You'll make the right call for yourself.

I know a lot about wine and I'm constantly learning more in my daily adventures with Girls Gone Grape, but for now I've chosen not to become a Sommelier. Maybe it's the little voice inside of me yelling at me not to become a wine snob because I know a few of those and I really don't enjoy being around them. After all, I started GGG to attract wine passionate gals who are just as happy with a $15 bottle of wine as they are a $250 bottle, because it's more about who they're drinking with than what they're drinking.

If you think you want to take the plunge, then I suggest checking out The International Wine Guild at www.internationalwineguild.com to see if they have a local location near you. There are online courses that can also be taken. They typically will allow self-study with your testing done at various locations and dates. You can also do a general search on the wonderful web to see if there are any other options near you. Good luck in your search and let us know if you become a Certified Sommelier!

> **"WHAT WINE GOES WITH CAPTAIN CRUNCH?"**
> **GEORGE CARLIN**

Closing/Finale – Your Wine Pack

As we come to the end of our sips together I hope you've had a few good laughs over the pages of this book as you've looked at your friends through a wine bottle or several glasses of wine! You're probably thinking several of your friends fit several of the wine types. That's awesome! Friends that fit into several wine types are your Blended Girlfriends! I love me some Blended Girlfriends because they keep life moving forward. I actually consider myself one of those Blended types because I see a bit of myself in all the wine types. Blended girlfriends round us out with just the right balance of each characteristic.

If this book touched your heart, the way I hoped it would, then right now you're thinking along the lines of:

- Wow. I need to call my best gal pal now!

- You're recognizing how important the girlfriends you call your pack, your wine club or your tribe are for your overall well-being.

- You're thinking you need to put more girl time into your calendar ASAP!

- You're wondering how quickly you can get that first Annual Girlfriends weekend going.

- You're in need of more wine!

Then fantastic! Salute, Sante, Salud, Cin Cin, Slainte, Prost, Cheers, etc.

Next, I'm going to invite you to join our Girls Gone Grape community and become a Girls Gone Grape Champagne Member for one year on me! We'll connect you with other gals who are sassy and passionate about wine and adventures and give you an insight into expanding your wine passion more. Use the coupon code below and head over to www.girlsgonegrape.com and join us today under the membership tab! You'll get our monthly Sip On Life, lifestyle digital magazine emailed directly to you along with access to fabulous wine tidbits! We're constantly adding more benefits and business partners monthly to keep you sipping with the gals and guys!

You'll have access to our member's area where you'll find awesome Business Partner offers along with Cellar Partner offers to enjoy. Look for local chapters and regional events being hosted by Girls Gone Grape. And, if you feel the tug at your heart and there isn't a chapter near you, reach out and let us tell you what it takes to bring a chapter to your city. Enjoy the sips with the girls because there are lots of stories to be told over empty bottles…

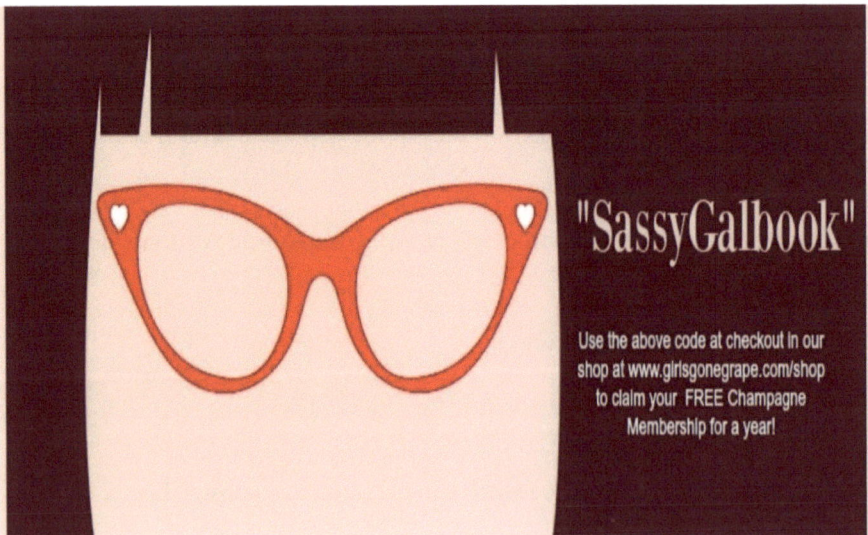

"SassyGalbook"

Use the above code at checkout in our shop at www.girlsgonegrape.com/shop to claim your FREE Champagne Membership for a year!

Bonus Perks

Throughout this book we've told you we'd include some items here in the back to help you in your sipping adventures with the gals!

We've provided pages here that you can copy and print with our permission to use with your girlfriends at your tastings. However, if you'd prefer them in PDF format, we'd be happy to send them to you by email if you request them over at info@girlsgonegrape.com. In the subject line just request GGG Book Perks and we'll send them all in one folder. Enjoy!

1) Sip It or Spill It Game – this is a mini version of our popular game. You'll get a copy of our board, limited game cards and directions for sipping through this game! Or, order the actual game and carry it around in your purse for just the right moment.

2) GGG Tasting Notes – this is a great sheet to provide during tasting for quick notes to take home of the wines you've enjoyed.

Other resources recommended to learn more:
www.winechanneltv.com
www.thechocolatetherapist.com
www.winefolly.com
www.vinepair.com
www.foodandwine.com
www.winespectator.com
www.winemag.com

The above are just a few of our "favorites."

Tasting Notes

Wine's Tasted Today:
1)
2)
3)
4)
5)

SEE -Note Wine Color & Clarity:
1)
2)
3)
4)
5)

SNIFF - Inhale. What aromoas do you pick up? Swirl and Sniff again. Did aromas change?
1)
2)
3)
4)
5)

SIP - Take a sip and slosh the wine across your tongue and note the flavor and texture.
1)
2)
3)
4)
5)

RATE - Would you purchase this wine?
1)
2)
3)
4)
5)

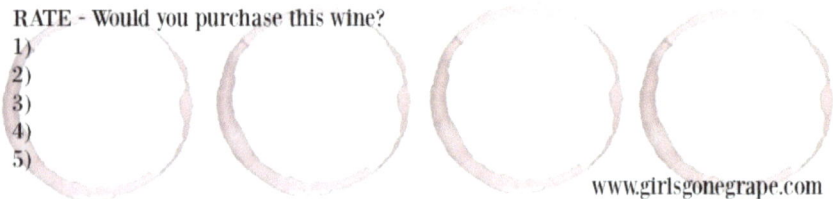

www.girlsgonegrape.com

Robin Salls

Sip It Or Spill It Game Board

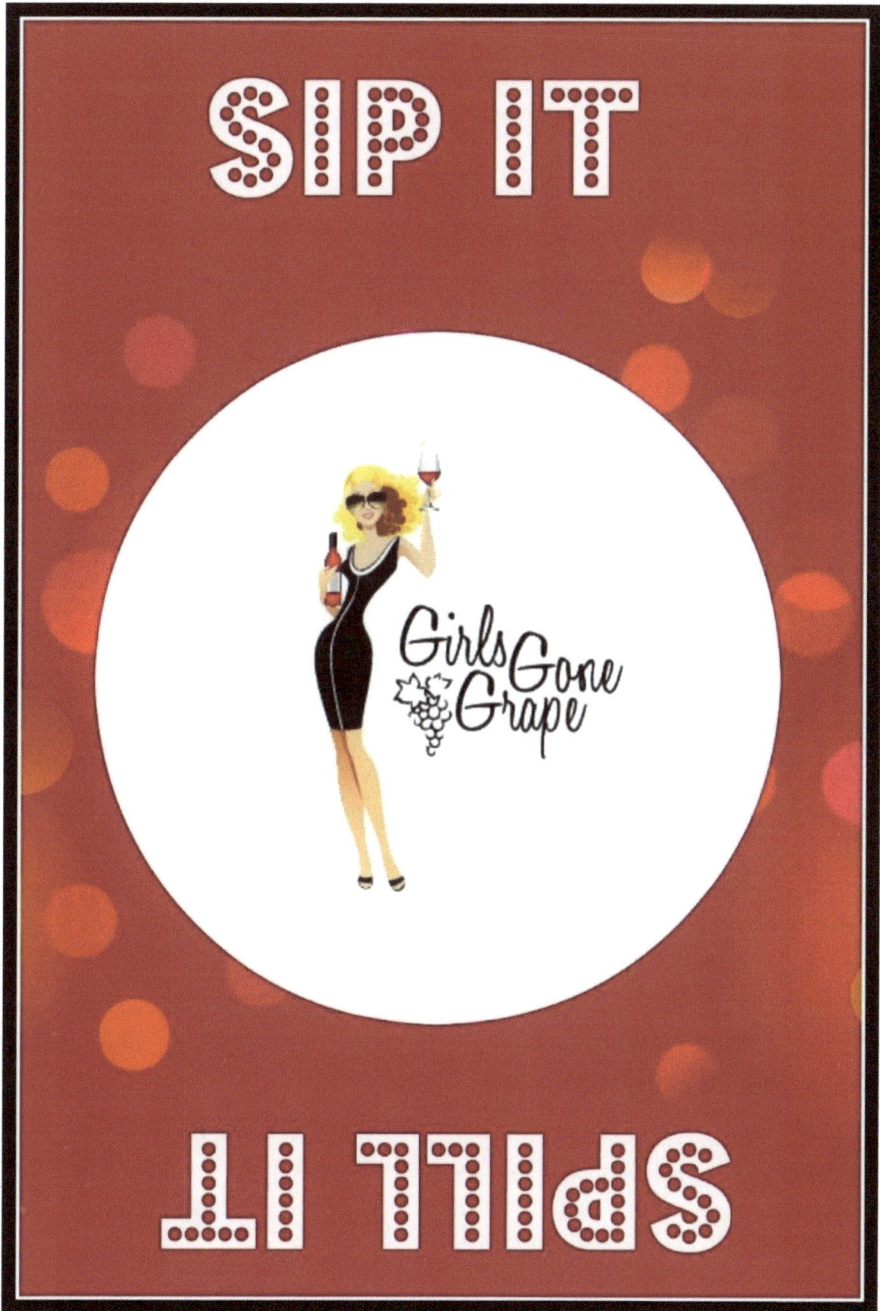

Sip It Cards

Show us your best yoga move while sipping your wine

SIP IT

Tell us in your sexiest voice "I'm a girl gone grape"

SIP IT

Give us your best stripper moves in 15 seconds

SIP IT

Flaunt your best asset for 15 seconds

SIP IT

Use the board on the previous page along with a mini Champagne bottle filled with sand or stone to spin the bottle and see which side it lands on. Sip It Cards are your "dare" cards for the GGG Sip It or Spill It game. This is a quick peak at our game that you can copy and give a try with your friends. It's just a sample of our dares, but to get the full game with lots of fun dares head over to our shop at www.girlsgonegrape.com.

Spill It Cards

Spill It Cards are your "truth" cards for the GGG Sip It or Spill It game. This is a quick peak at our game that you can copy and give a try with your friends. It's just a sample of our truths, but to get the full game with lots of fun truths to share, head over to our shop at www.girlsgonegrape.com.

About The Author

Robin is passionate about connecting and inspiring women to reach out to one another and lift each other up. Her entrepreneur spirit has led her on a journey venturing in sales, marketing, radio, writing and non-profits while always following her passion. It is this lust for living "La Dolce Vita" (a sweet life) that has culminated in the founding of Girls Gone Grape, Inc. where she combines all her passions.

She's a woman who throws out the map and takes the road less travelled by choice. She lives in Colorado with her husband David and their four fur kids; Jax, Lulu, Sheldon and Sangria. Robin loves traveling and introducing Girls Gone Grape chapters as she finds you can never sip enough wine or share enough with others. When not sipping wine, you'll likely find her adventuring outdoors or helping others live their passion. She adores everything Italian, especially the way the Italians value family, food and wine. And, yes, she admits she's a bit bias because of her Italian heritage.

Robin speaks regularly to groups of all kinds including women's groups, men's groups, luncheons, corporations, non-profits, and more. To book a speaking engagement or private event, contact Robin at **robin@girlsgonegrape.com**.

www.girlsgonegrape.com
@girlsgonegrape   #girlsgonegrape

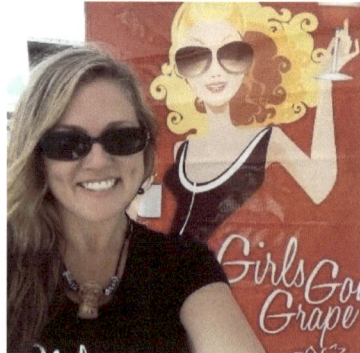